Clearing the Way to Awakening

Companion Workbook

Your Ngondro Process

Yudron Wangmo

ARROW
OF LOVE

Copyright © 2025 by Yudron Wangmo

All Rights Reserved

No part of this book may be used or reproduced by any means, graphic, electronic, or mechanical, including photocopying, recording, taping, or by any information storage retrieval system, without the written permission of the publisher, except in the case of brief quotations embodied in critical articles and reviews.

Arrow of Love Publications
1996 Quiver Street
Copperopolis, CA 95228

The Crimson Pro font is copyright © 2018 The Crimson Pro Project Authors
The Nunito font is copyright © 2014 The Nunito Project Authors

All illustrations were A.I. generated.

ISBN: 978-0-9969241-8-4

Table of Contents

Introduction..i
1. Aspiration... 1
2. Reorientation... 7
3. Appreciation.. 11
4. Deterioration.. 14
5. Dissatisfaction.. 22
6. Repercussions.. 24
7. Exploration.. 33
8. Accumulation... 36
9. Representation... 40
10. Interconnection.. 44
11. Protection... 49
12. Motivation.. 53
13. Purification... 57
14. Multiplication... 60
15. Unification.. 68
16. Integration.. 76
Conclusion... 81

Introduction

This book is for you if you have received a ngondro practice from a representative of a Tibetan Buddhist tradition and are getting started. The main book, *Clearing the Way to Awakening*, gives you the why, what, and how of each step. Now comes the exciting experience of practicing ngondro in your real life! That's what this workbook is about.

Just knowing that you are out there sincerely practicing ngondro inspires me. Let's face it, it's a special group of people who are interested in Vajrayana Buddhism who were not born into it. A subset of that group who wants to do a serious amount of practice each day in order to truly experience the transformation it brings. You've made that life-changing decision to practice.

If you are like me, your life will never be the same.

Now that you've started—or are about to start—you'll find you have new questions. A senior student or teacher can give some of them routine answers. But many are about your personal process. Those can only be answered from within you, through a wide-open process of self-inquiry.

This workbook will help with:

- Creating a personal record of who you were when you started ngondro, so you can see your amazing transformation after completing the accumulations.
- Sparking personal insights and not discounting or forgetting them.
- Integrate practice with household life.
- Consistently engaging with the mind trainings in the outer ngondro so they truly become a part of you.
- Forming a heartfelt connection with imagery that might initially feel unfamiliar.
- Getting clear on questions that often arise only once you begin practicing.
- Finding ongoing support on your journey.

This workbook encourages you to move beyond passively listening to dharma teachings or skimming Dharma books. Instead, use the questions and exercises in this workbook to truly go deeper. Ngondro is profoundly personal, and I know you'll have different "aha!" moments and unique insights than I did, based on your own experience.

Many Tibetan and Bhutanese lamas have memorized the outline of Patrul Rinpoche's *Words of My Perfect Teacher*, and even entire passages. When questions come up, it's as if they're entering a search term into a mental database to find a solution… or perhaps from texts like Gampopa's *Jewel Ornament of Liberation* as well. If we were educated in secular schools, we aren't accustomed to learning this way. We've been exposed to scientific and psychological ideas that emphasize critical thinking and personal inquiry. Because of these differences, I believe ngondro is actually *more crucial* for us than it is in traditional Asian societies.

Whether you practice daily or not, whether your sessions are long or short, ngondro is physically and emotionally intense. I think this intensity and speed helps spark a whole-hearted practice with both joys and pain points along the way.

Understanding Different Approaches to Authority

It may be helpful for you to consider the cultural contexts that shape our approach to spiritual practice. In traditional Tibetan society, relationships with authority figures—especially those in the religious sphere—are often characterized by a hierarchical structure, reverence, and loyalty.

- Lamas aren't just teachers; they're often seen as spiritual parents or embodiments of awakened mind. This fosters deep trust, obedience, and sometimes idealization.
- Authority is typically inherited or spiritually conferred, and people don't easily question it.
- Traditional Tibetan culture emphasizes collectivism. People prioritize maintaining harmony and honoring their role in the social fabric, which includes obedience to elders and teachers.

In contrast, people in the U.S., for example, often have a very different relationship to authority:

- Individualism: American culture is rooted in ideas of personal freedom, self-determination, and skepticism of hierarchy. We're encouraged to question authority, forge our own path, and "think for ourselves."
- Christian Influence: While Christianity also has hierarchies (priests, ministers), Protestantism, in particular, introduced a more personal, direct relationship with the divine.
- Cultural Diversity and Pluralism: In the U.S., authority is often fragmented across many competing systems—religious, secular, academic, etc.—which encourages debate and choice rather than blind loyalty.
- Trauma and Suspicion: Especially in recent decades, awareness of abuse or exploitation in religious or institutional settings has led many to be cautious, even cynical, about surrendering to clerical authority.

A Space for Exploration

In traditional Tibetan Buddhist settings, when someone has a question about ngondro practice, they naturally go to their lama. The teacher listens, perhaps asks a few questions, and then gives a clear answer. The student usually accepts that answer without much debate. This is how it works in a culture where people grow up trusting their teachers and following the ways of their ancestors.

But if you grew up in a place strongly influenced by Christian European colonization, as I did, things might feel different. You may not feel comfortable simply doing what someone says, especially if it doesn't make sense yet. Perhaps you've been hurt by authority figures in the past, or maybe you simply learn best through your own experiences.

I create my books with you in mind. It's here to help you explore your own thoughts and feelings. It offers you a space to reflect, experiment, and ask honest questions about the path you're walking.

Ngondro is about clearing the way—inside your heart and mind—so that awakening becomes possible. That's a significant journey, and it's perfectly okay if you need to take your time with it. When I hear from people who give up ngondro practice, it seems like some of them didn't feel they could show up for it as their authentic selves. Feelings bubbled up and became intolerable.

These pages offer a space to be real with yourself. I encourage you to bring your whole self—your doubts, your insights, and everything in between—into the process. No one else has to see what you write here. However, I believe that by showing up honestly, you'll find clarity begins to emerge from within.

I'm an American woman who has completed three ngondros and deeply practiced with three others. My lamas didn't require all of these. As I mentioned in *Clearing the Way*, I truly found that I loved ngondro, and I hope you come to love it too.

Please know that I'm out here in the California countryside, rooting for you. Even if you read this after my time, feel that my support is still with you.

Chapter 1

Aspiration

What Draws You Here?

There are endless ways to spend a human life, so why are you here? Why sit down with a practice that demands so much of your time and attention when the world is full of quicker pleasures, louder distractions, and perhaps even more urgent demands?

I believe something inside you brought you here—a spark, some questions, or perhaps a deep longing for freedom. This section is about creating space to connect with that inner pull. What's truly pulling you toward this path?

Pick up a pen. Let's get started.

Reflection Prompts
- What made you want to pick up this book or workbook in the first place?
- When you imagine yourself doing ngondro practice, or are really doing it, how do you feel? Excited, sceptical, curious, resistant?
- If you had to describe what you're looking for in one sentence, what would it be?

Journaling Space: What's Stirring in You?

Use this space to write freely. Try not to edit or judge what comes up.

"What is driving my interest in ngondro... down deep?"

_____
_____
_____

Sit with the Spark

Find a comfortable seat. Ask yourself, gently: Why do I want to practice?
Don't force an answer. Just notice what arises. Sit with that for a few minutes

What Does Awakening Mean to You?

I think it's worth repeating that the word Buddha means "awakened one." Buddha isn't a god, nor is the state of awakening a concept, plan, or opinion. The Tibetan language adds something beautiful to this idea: their word for awakening means purified and expanded. It suggests that everything clouded or tight has been cleared away, leaving what's wide open, bright, kind, clear, and capable.

You don't need to become someone else. Instead, awakening involves removing what covers your natural wisdom so that what has always been there can shine through. While I'm writing this in the style of a self-help book, I want you to avoid the idea that something is inherently wrong with you. Many of us tend to think this way about ourselves, as if we have a congenital illness that requires a diagnosis before treatment can begin.

Yet, there is an oft-stated analogy that your lama is like a skilled physician, and following his or her advice is like taking medicine. At the same time, though, underneath that illness of samsara you are fundamentally okay. While these may seem contradictory, together they indicate that your buddhanature never gets sick, and your lama will help you find that place of peaceful, open clarity.

Reflect
- What comes to mind when you hear the word "awakening"?
- Do you believe this kind of inner shift is possible for you, or others?
- Is there something right with you when you look deeply at yourself?

Where We Are Now: Noticing the Mess Without Shame

You're probably undertaking ngondro because something in your life isn't quite settled. Something in you deeply desires clarity, steadiness, and peace.

In the Buddhist view, being an ordinary sentient being simply means you haven't yet fully seen through the habits of confusion, especially the tightness of clinging and the constant swirl of opinion-making. We all experience this as part of the human condition. The good news is that simply seeing the current status of our mind clearly is already a significant step toward freedom.

Reflection Prompts
- What's one recent example of your mind sticking to a story, label, or judgment… like a dog's jaw clenched around a special toy?
- How do your thoughts shape your emotions, or stir up reactions?
- When you imagine letting go of mental chatter or judgments, how does that feel— scary, spacious, strange, wonderful?

Watching the Mind Work

If you've never tried *shamatha* calm abiding practice, I recommend giving it a go. It's a great way to simply notice how your conceptual mind constantly tries to reassert itself.

- Sit comfortably, with your eyes open or closed.
- Gently bring your attention to your breath.
- When a thought arises, simply notice it.
- Just observe it without fighting it.
- Then, gently return to your breath.

Practice this for a few minutes from time to time. It's a wonderful way to become more friendly with your own human mind.

The Storehouse Consciousness

Buddhist teachings describe the storehouse consciousness, or *alaya vijnana*, as a kind of mental basement. It's where our past intentions, reactions, and patterns leave their mark. These underpinnings don't disappear, even when we've forgotten them. They actively shape how we show up in the world, moment by moment.

When we engage in spiritual practice, we're doing more than just learning new habits. We're actively scrubbing this inner basement—clearing, transforming, and even liberating what's been locked up there. This is what purification truly means.

Reflection
- When you look at your reactions or habits, do any feel older than this lifetime—or at least older than your conscious memory?
- Have you ever noticed a repetitive emotional pattern, that you know is not helpful?

Journaling Space: What's Been Stored?

Use this space to reflect on your inner conditioning.

One emotional habit I keep returning to is:

_____
_____
_____
_____
_____

Sometimes I feel like I was shaped by...

_____
_____
_____
_____
_____

I'd love to clear out the part of me that keeps on…"

_____
_____
_____
_____
_____

Guided Practice: Imagining the Storehouse

1. Sit quietly and picture a spacious room inside you.
2. Imagine it holds all your old habits—some heavy, some light.
3. Without judging, notice what the room feels like.
4. Imagine opening a big window. Let fresh air flow in.
5. Sit for a minute with the sense of space and possibility.

Write words or draw pictures inside the sumo wrestler's chest that remind you of your storehouse consciousness.

Wrapping Up: Starting the Shift

You don't have to run off to a cave or pretend to be someone else to accomplish ngondro. This practice invites you to shift into a new way of relating to your life and your world. I see these nine trainings as working like a powerful reset button—a way to gently, steadily start clearing out old programming from the inside out.

You are truly becoming a serious practitioner. Welcome! I'm excited for you.

Chapter 2

Reorientation

Reflecting on Your Current Outlook

If you're early in your outer ngondro practice, I suggest taking a moment to consider your current beliefs about the big "meaning-of-life" questions addressed by the traditional *four contemplations that turn the mind*, which come at the beginning of your text. I've provided some journaling prompts below to help you get honest about the stories and assumptions that might be running in the background of your mind.

For each contemplation, jot down a few thoughts or beliefs you currently hold, without editing or judging. These might be beliefs you were raised with, conclusions drawn from your experience, or simply how things feel to you at this moment.

The Value of This Life
What do you believe about your life's potential? For example, do you see it as meaningful? Limited? Full of opportunities? Too hard?
My current view:

_____
_____
_____
_____
_____

Impermanence
How do you feel about the fact that people, things, and situations change or end? Is this something you think about much? Avoid? Accept? Resist?
My current view:

_____
_____
_____
_____
_____

The Nature of Suffering

Why do people (including you) suffer? Do you think suffering is avoidable? Fair? Random? Deserved? Just part of life?

My current view:

_____
_____
_____
_____
_____

Karma / Cause and Effect

What do you believe about consequences? Do your actions have long-term impact beyond the obvious ones? Are outcomes mostly due to luck, effort, or something else? Do past positive and negative actions affect you now or in your future lives?

My current view:

_____
_____
_____
_____
_____

Your Practice Space and Posture

The space you create for your ngondro practice is truly important. To practice well, you need a place, a time, a seat, and a clear mindset. Before you begin reflecting deeply or chanting mantras, you'll make small but necessary decisions about where and how you practice. This section helps you establish those foundations. I encourage you to try each of these exercises to create a setup that works for your body, your household, and your mind.

Claim Your Space: Create a Designated Practice Area

Look around your living space and identify a quiet, minimally trafficked location, such as a corner of a room. If you live with others (human or animal), I suggest you ask them to respect this space during your sessions.

Consider what kind of shrine you'd like: a traditional ngondro shrine, a minimal and discreet one, or no shrine at all. If you opt for something minimal, simply place a visual reminder there that this area is for spiritual work—perhaps a photo, with a fresh flower, or a nice bottle of water. Keep it clean and pleasant, and as free from visual distractions as you can.

Pro tip: If you usually use a tablet or phone for your text, I encourage you to experiment with printing out the prayers or visualizations instead. That way, you won't have the allure of social media and messages right in your face.

What's the atmosphere of this space? What helps you feel focused or at ease here?

_____
_____
_____
_____

Check In with Your Inspiration: Light the Fire

Before each session, pause for a moment and ask yourself: "Why am I practicing today?"

Recall something that initially inspired you—perhaps a teacher, a teaching, an insight, or a story. If you have a teacher who recommended ngondro to you, remember their words.

Notice how reconnecting with your "why" changes your energy.

Work with Your Body

If you're unfamiliar with seated meditation practice, you'll find instructions for a seating setup in the main book.

After sitting for 15–20 minutes, I encourage you to check in: what is your body telling you? Do your knees hover above the floor mat? Does discomfort increase over time? If so, consider adjusting your seat height or incorporating regular hip and leg stretches. If necessary, please sit in a chair—or even lie down—without any guilt or judgment.

What position allows you to sit still and alert, without pain?

Working with the Day's Energy

Calming Agitation

When your mind feels wild, try not to fight it. Instead, I suggest these approaches:
Speak directly to your mind: "We'll take care of those tasks soon. Let's just practice for now."
Make a short list of anything urgent your mind keeps bringing up. This can help release it.
Experiment with darkening the room, sitting lower, or eating something a bit heavier before practice.

Optional experiment:
Cut back on coffee or switch to tea for a few days. See how it affects your mind during sessions.

Lifting Drowsiness

If you find yourself nodding off during practice:

- Ask yourself honestly if you're getting enough sleep at night.
- Try practicing in a brighter room, sitting up higher, or eating lighter beforehand.
- Lift your gaze slightly or open your eyes a bit more.

Wrap-Up: Let It Be Simple

You don't have to run away from home or pretend to be someone else to accomplish ngondro. Your practice space doesn't need to be fancy, and you don't need a perfect body. What truly matters is that you sit down, connect with your intention, and work with what's real for you right now. Please be kind to yourself, and keep showing up.

Chapter 3

Appreciation: Contemplation of the Precious Human Life

Why This Life Matters

This chapter introduces a core premise of the Buddhist path: the opportunity you have right now is truly extraordinary. You may not always feel fortunate, but from the perspective of the Dharma, your current human life most likely possesses uncommon qualities that make deep transformation possible.

The classical teaching on precious human birth describes eighteen factors—eight freedoms and ten endowments—that create a life conducive to liberation. The main point is this: it's rare to be born as a human, with enough freedom from constant hardship and enough inner clarity to even consider the Dharma. It's even rarer to encounter authentic teachings and genuinely care about awakening.

Take a Moment to Reflect

When did you first become aware that spiritual practice might be important in your life?

_____
_____
_____
_____
_____

What aspects of your current situation support your ability to reflect, meditate, or study the Dharma?

_____
_____
_____
_____
_____

Are there any freedoms or advantages you've taken for granted that now seem significant?

_____
_____
_____
_____

Reflection:

How does it affect you to be told that this life is scarce and meaningful?
If you truly accepted that this opportunity might not come again, how might that change your approach to practice?
What distractions tend to pull you away from Dharma? How might you respond differently if you knew the stakes?

Facing Resistance and Forgetfulness

Even when we're clear about the extraordinary opportunity we have, we still forget. We get tired, distracted, or discouraged. This section offers you space to acknowledge those patterns and gently work with them.

We aren't "bad" practitioners because we lose sight of our intention, especially in the beginning. This is precisely why reflecting on the precious human life needs to be a repeated practice, something we actively engage with. The more deeply we see the truth of our opportunity, the more naturally our motivation returns.

You might also encounter deeper forms of resistance: old doubts, unconscious fears. These are simply habits of thought. You can change them. Reflection Prompts:

- What usually causes you to drift away from your intention to practice?
- What beliefs about yourself might be limiting your engagement with the Dharma?
- What helps you reconnect with your sense of inspiration?

Committing to the Path

If this life is as rare and powerful as the teachings describe, how will you choose to use it? This section is about making a personal commitment to something alive in you right now.

You don't have to know everything about Buddhism. And, while advanced retreats and fancy rituals have value, what truly matters is that you orient your life around awakening. I find that the path naturally unfolds step by step. All it requires is resolve, sincerity, and continuity.

Over time, people who value their precious human birth gradually begin to guard their time, choose meaningful activities, and let Dharma shape their priorities.

Reflection:

To help you clarify your commitment, consider these questions:

- ☞ What, specifically, does committing to this path mean for you at this point in your life?
- ☞ Is there anything you're ready to let go of in order to protect your intention?
- ☞ How will you remind yourself of the preciousness of this opportunity when you forget?

Optional Practice:

Make a simple, personal vow. It might be as short as: "May I not waste this life's precious opportunity." Write it down and keep it somewhere visible for a week.

Chapter 4

Deterioration

You will have both a happier life and a deeper understanding of what "emptiness" means if you come to truly accept that everything in life has a beginning and an ending. Knowing that everything is changeable and impermanent helps loosen our chains of attachment to people, places, objects, and circumstances. This awareness of the lack of inherent solidity in ourselves and the world reduces our clinginess to "our people." It also lessens our hatred of those we see as adversaries. In the long term, it sparks a genuine passion for doing good in the world while we still can.

I believe this single practice of contemplating impermanence can lead to both recognizing your pristine consciousness (yeshe) and creating an intensely positive trajectory for your life.

Journaling Prompt

When in your life has remembering that something won't last helped you appreciate it more deeply or get through it? Use this space to write freely — don't worry about sounding wise or getting it "right." Just let the memory or experience come through.

Write for five minutes without stopping about the feeling of letting go of something you once clung to.

_____
_____
_____
_____
_____
_____
_____
_____
_____
_____
_____

Exploring a Zillion-year Time Perspective

What opens up in your perspective when you try to hold the "big view" of this point in the expanse of time? What seems less important? What suddenly matters more?

_____
_____
_____
_____

Obstacles to the Practice: Managing Fear and Anxiety

We often reach a point in spiritual practice where the very thing we need to look at most deeply also stirs discomfort, fear, or resistance. When it comes to impermanence, that barrier is often anxiety. I invite you to meet that with gentleness, honesty, and skill.

Gentle Ways to Begin Awareness of Impermanence

If you want to ease into this practice:

- ★ Notice small changes: your breath, the moving light and shadows of the sun's journey through the day, the sound of a bird call.
- ★ Recite a simple line like "This too is passing" during your day.
- ★ End each day with this reflection: What changed today? What stayed the same?
- ★ Let your mind warm up to the idea of impermanence like dipping your toes in the lake to check the temperature before jumping.

Reflection: Letting Go of Half-Truths

When I think about it, I see that most of us were taught how to chase after what we want and avoid what we don't. You probably got good at it, and so did I. But underneath all that effort, something else is always happening. The change that is always beyond our control

Everything has a natural arc: a beginning, a middle, and an end. People, animals, plants, houses, bodies, moods, the buzz of a phone in your pocket, the aftertaste of tea, the smell of a room after someone leaves it—all of it arises and fades. Our brightest insights and our darkest days are on their way out even as they show up.

This first level of insight into impermanence involves unlearning that old storyline, the fairy tale that promises: "If you work hard, or get lucky, or figure it out, lasting happiness will be yours." Thinking that way sets us up for a thousand little heartbreaks from life's unpredictable ups and downs.

Journaling Exercise

Describe a time when the impermanence of something (a season, a feeling, a relationship) was a painful realization, and then a liberating one.

_____
_____
_____
_____
_____

What you Might Be Noticing

We were taught that if you do it right, you get to keep what you love.
The world itself whispers a different truth: Nothing stays.
This insight isn't a cause for despair; it's a profound chance to stop living a lie.

Journal Reflection

Who were the people who shaped your early ideas about success and happiness? What did they emphasize—achievement, romance, money, fitting in

_____
_____
_____
_____
_____

Write down one moment from your life where something you wanted did come to you... and then left. What was the experience of its leaving like?

Think of a time when something that seemed terrible ended or changed unexpectedly. Do you see the situation differently now?

Accepting that everything has an arc doesn't diminish life. Instead, it makes each moment shine more sharply, like morning sunlight after a storm. This is where the work of freedom begins—when we learn how to ride change with grace, rather than trying to transcend it.

The Inevitability of Illness

For many of us, the COVID-19 pandemic cracked open our illusion of permanence. In those early days, time stopped in its tracks. That sudden silence—familiar routines gone, the future uncertain—was a true wake-up call. Even now, years later, those memories can still stir something within us. I invite you to consider: What was revealed when the old structures paused for you? This was a shared experience.

Epidemic and sudden illnesses remind us we are not in control. They interrupt our personal storylines. They give us an urgent opportunity: to prepare, to practice, to wake up.

Journal Reflection

What do you remember about the first days of the pandemic? How did it affect your body, your mind, your sense of time? Did you feel uncertainty about whether or not you would survive? What came up? Panic, relief, numbness, resolve, curiosity? Have you ever treated a practice session like a rehearsal for death? If not, what do you imagine that might feel like?

_____
_____
_____
_____

Every reminder of our vulnerability to illness can also be a doorway to "getting" impermanence.

Facing up to Aging

Aging is visible. It appears in the mirror, in the stories we tell about our aches and energies, and in how others perceive and treat us. It also unfolds invisibly: deep inside, in the cellular processes quietly rearranging us every moment. We can use this time to meet these realities with curiosity and honesty.

Reflection

Take a few moments to become still. Sit where you can be near a mirror. Relax your gaze and simply look, without judgment. Observe the texture of your skin, the color and texture of your hair, and all of the features of your body. Note the judgments that arise in your mind from comparing how your body looks now with how it looked in the past, or how someone else looks. Just tag them as thoughts and let them move on. Remain fresh and present.

Now consider: How long has this body been alive? What has it survived, adapted to, carried you through? Are you 100% the same person you were ten, twenty, or thirty years ago? If you had lived in a different place and time, without antibiotics or emergency medicine, would you have survived until now? Be with things as they are in this moment.

Close your session by patting your own shoulder with your opposite hand. Say "Atta boy," or "Atta girl," congratulating yourself on your willingness to relate to yourself and the world in an utterly new way. Whether you are twenty or ninety, you are undergoing a profound shift.

The Aging Body is a Teacher

In Buddhist practice, aging isn't seen as a problem to be solved. Instead, it's a truth to be known intimately. Looking in the mirror as your body changes can be a powerful reminder to not fritter away our time on superficial pursuits.

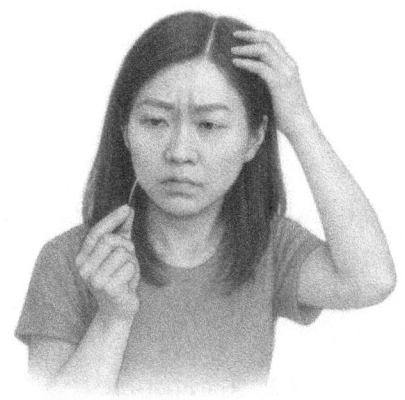

Reflection
- What stories have you inherited about aging? From your family? From your culture? Which ones still influence you?
- Have you ever tried to "outrun" aging through lifestyle, speech, or self-image? What was behind that?
- Can you recall a moment when you felt at peace with growing older, or saw someone else embody that acceptance?
- If your body is always changing, what do you believe is always present throughout?

Acceptance of the Inevitability of Death

Your life—this life—is impermanent. That's not news, of course. Yet, the way we live, plan, and speak suggests that most of us live our lives hoping we can blink and the prospect of death will simply disappear.

Today, I invite you not to turn away. To overcome the denial that is constantly reasserting itself.

Death isn't merely a distant event at the end of life. Every ending is a little death; the last breath of a conversation, the crumpling of a leaf, the breaking down of a thought. Yet, for most of us, the idea of our own death remains strangely abstract—something to avoid or delay rather than live with as a teacher.

This reflection invites you to turn toward it.

Death rarely makes an appointment. Even if you receive notice in the form of illness or age, the actual moment of departure is unknown. And yet, how much of your day is spent as if you were guaranteed another one? Reflect on these traditional Buddhist practice prompts.

Reflection
- How do you typically respond to thoughts about your own death? Fear? Detachment? Curiosity?
- Are there ways you avoid facing mortality, perhaps through constant busyness, or refusing to make end-of-life plans?
- Can you recall a time when death—or the nearness of it—brought clarity to your priorities?
- What, if anything, do you want to complete or express before you die?

A Mini Rehearsal

Set a timer for 10–15 minutes. Sit quietly and imagine this is your final hour of life. Let go of plans, worries, and even aspirations. Reflect:

- What actually matters now?
- Will anything be deathless?

When the timer ends, stand up slowly and re-enter your day. Let the experience guide how you spend your next few hours.

The Great Boon of Bearing One's Own Death in Mind

Reflecting on our own death is about claiming our lives. When we allow the knowledge of impermanence to truly sink in, the extraneous falls away. Our priorities are clarified, and the urgency to engage with what genuinely matters intensifies. For me, this awareness has been a catalyst, shifting me from a state of perpetual preparation to one of active, appreciative living. It's the ultimate reminder to step into each moment with both tenderness and fierce dedication, knowing its fleeting beauty.

Accepting Impermanence Will Change You

Acceptance of impermanence is a core teaching of the Buddha. For example, it is one of the Four Seals, a set of axioms that define Buddhism:

- All compounded things are impermanent.
- All contaminated things are suffering.
- All phenomena are empty and devoid of self.
- Nirvana is true peace.

Future You will be very interested in how you are wrapping your head around impermanence now, and how you hope to more deeply integrate this recognition as a practitioner. Let's close this chapter with a message in a bottle.

Letter to My Future Self

Write a letter to your future self, 10 years from now, reflecting on your current relationship with impermanence. What wisdom do you hope to have gained?

_____
_____
_____
_____
_____
_____
_____
_____
_____
_____
_____
_____
_____
_____
_____
_____
_____

Chapter 5

Dissatisfaction

Facing Dukkha

Buddha promised that an end to suffering is possible. And it is demonstrably true: our pain the "afflictions" do subside when we practice systematically and regularly and understand why we are doing what we are doing. It is truly amazing. Without understanding and acknowledging the pain of ourselves and others, we would be both unmotivated to practice and unable to spot our transformation.

It's easy to believe that if we just get things right, life should be smooth. If you've ever felt that pain means you've messed up, or that you've somehow failed to manifest something better, please know this: This is the nature of life. You're not being punished.

We learned, in so many subtle and not-so-subtle ways, that if we just worked hard enough, stayed positive, were kind, ate right, and didn't rock the boat, the universe owed us a reward—a life free from pain.

We still get sick. Lose our jobs. People we care deeply about might betray us, or disappear from our lives. Our bodies will age and ache. Our minds can take wild, unbidden turns.

And yes, it really hurts.

In Buddhism, the ancient Pali word *dukkha* points to this vast, sometimes unsettling, territory of human experience. It encompasses obvious pain and sorrow, but also a more subtle sense of dissatisfaction, stress, or a deep-down unease. It's that feeling that things are never quite right, that life can feel a little off-kilter, even in moments we might call successful or joyful.

When we begin to look at this dukkha directly, that's when clarity truly begins to emerge. We start to see not only the nature of our pain, but also, importantly, the profound possibility of genuine freedom from suffering.

This approach is about meeting pain and difficult feelings head-on, with a different kind of wisdom.

Reflection: What Do You Add to the Pain?

We've all had moments of raw discomfort—an illness, a loss, a betrayal. And then there are the stories we told ourselves about it. "This shouldn't be happening." "Why me?" "I'll never get through this."

This thinking creates a second layer of pain: the suffering about suffering.

Take a moment to think of a painful event in your life. It doesn't need to be the worst one.

What actually happened? (Just the facts—without the storyline.)

What were the initial thoughts and emotions that arose in direct response to the facts?

Looking back, what did you add to that pain with the story you told yourself about it? What beliefs or interpretations of yours caused that additional pain?

Journaling Prompt:

Write a few sentences starting with: "If I could guarantee one thing never changed, it would be..."

_____
_____
_____
_____

Then ask yourself: what would the cost of that be?

_____
_____

Mini Rehearsals for Change

Sit down for a little while and imagine one thing in your life changing—something you usually rely on or enjoy. You don't need to go for worst-case scenarios. Just enough to notice resistance.

Where do you feel that resistance in your body? What is that sensation saying to you? Is there an underlying thought or opinion? Experiment with staying present with the reality you are presented with, rather than your interpretation of it.

Repeat with another small change. This is gentle exposure. You're training your mind to stay open and relaxed when things don't go your way.

Do you ever catch yourself repeating a pattern and think, "I don't even know why I do this"?

_____
_____
_____

Chapter 6

Repercussions

Reflecting on Karma and Its Effects

We've all heard someone say, "That's karma," usually when something ironic or harsh happens to someone they don't like. Karma is a natural law of cause and effect that shapes our experience, moment by moment, life after life. What if mindfulness of karma can shape our future situation more effectively than careful planning can?

You've probably noticed that in Buddhist cultures, karma isn't an abstract theory. It's something people live with in a practical, down-to-earth way. Each small act, even a kind glance or a moment of patience, is seen as a seed with the power to ripen later—maybe much later. Past actions shape our current experience, and what we do now influences our future. This applies just as much to mental states as it does to outward deeds.

How is this way of thinking beginning to settle within you?

Reflecting on Karma

Journaling Prompts

What does "karma" mean to you right now?

___

___

___

Have you seen the ripple effects of someone's actions—positive or negative—expand outward through a community or a family? Try to trace the long tail of a real-life example you've witnessed or heard about.

___

___

___

What does that suggest about how actions shape our world?

___

___

What kind of skepticism do you carry about karma, rebirth, or the continuation of consciousness after death? Don't shy away from doubt—write it out clearly. Consider where it comes from. Is it based on personal experience? Scientific worldview? Distrust of dogma?

_____

_____

_____

Reflection Exercise: The Chain Reaction

Our consciousness is like an unbroken chain. Each link affects the next. Label the links of the chain below. Start with a choice you made this week—what were its effects? What was the state of mind behind it? Keep following the links. Where did it take you, and how might it continue?

Label the Links in the Chain

Contemplation Practice: Life Beyond This One?

Sit quietly for a few minutes and reflect: What if your consciousness does continue after death? Experiment with imagining that. Let yourself feel how this possibility might shift the way you live now.

Are you willing to proceed from here with the conviction that karma is a fact, even though it cannot be proven scientifically?

Ethics in Action: Shaping Your Karmic Path

Journaling Prompt

What's your reaction to the idea of consciously making decisions about your life and actions with karma in mind? Does that feel natural? Challenging? A stretch? A relief? What's your current relationship with ethical choices? Have you been trying to avoid harm, or do you sometimes justify certain behaviours as being "not that bad"? What guides your decisions now?

_____
_____
_____
_____
_____
_____
_____
_____
_____
_____

Anger and Skillful Conflict

Buddhist training sometimes assumes that if you understand karma deeply enough, you'll naturally avoid harming others. But emotional maturity also requires learning how to navigate difficult conversations.

Pick one recent interpersonal conflict. Write about how it unfolded and how you handled it. Then reflect: Did I communicate with clarity? Or, was there some aggression or passive aggression?

What would a more skilful response look like—one that neither denies the conflict nor communicates aggression or disrespect?

_____
_____
_____
_____
_____
_____

Write a short script of what you wish you'd said. Consider practicing it aloud.

_____
_____
_____
_____
_____
_____

Cultivating Positive Conduct

Motivation Check: What Drives My Good Deeds?

In Mahayana Buddhism, our inner motivation is paramount. A generous action done to impress others doesn't plant the same karmic seed as one done to benefit others.

Reflect on a few recent good deeds. For example, refraining from anger at a co-worker and helping them instead, saving a spider by taking it outside, or taking time to speak to someone who is down on their luck. For each one, write the action, and then try to be honest about the motivation behind it.

Action	What was my true motivation?	Was it to benefit others, myself, or both?

Core Focus Exercise: Refraining from Killing

Recall a moment when you killed an animal or insect, or approved of someone else doing so (even casually).

- What were you feeling at the time?
- Was there any reflection about the pain and death of the being at the time
- How did you feel afterward?

Describe that moment and how you feel about it now.

_____
_____
_____

Four Elements of a Fully-Formed Karma of Killing

According to Buddhist analysis, an act of killing becomes especially heavy if four elements are present:

1. You recognize the being is alive
2. You feel aversion or attachment toward it
3. You intentionally take its life
4. You feel pleased about its death

Think of a moment when you killed from your past. Were all four elements present? How might you have altered the situation to reduce karmic impact?

Life-Protecting Actions

Make a list of 3–5 realistic things you could do in your life to actively protect life, either human or animal. Include at least one that could become a habit, not just a one-time act.

_____
_____
_____
_____
_____

A Weekly Plan for Positive Karma (from the Karmavibhanga)

The vast perspective of Vajrayana Buddhism de-emphasizes black-and-white judgments and universal rules of conduct.

However, since many of us are new to Buddhism altogether, let's go over the Buddha's words in the Karmavibhanga, a text from early Buddhism. This sutra offers straightforward yet profound guidance on how to avoid negative karmic deeds and cultivate positive karma. Like a timeless influencer, the Buddha provides quick reminders of specific things we can do regarding non-harming & life-saving, practicing generosity, acts of kindness, refraining from ripping off others, and cultivating an uplifted, compassionate life.

Acts of Non-Harming and Life-Saving

- Promote and encourage the avoidance of killing.
- Speak out in support of those who promote non-killing and harm reduction.
- Actively save lives.
- Protect others from scary situations.
- Praise people who refrain from physical violence.

- ✌ Reflect on how wonderful it is when people settle disputes non-violently.
- ✌ Reject war.

Acts of Generosity

- ❀ Be generous.
- ❀ Make offerings to the Three Jewels: drinks, garlands, flowers, lights, incense, and food.
- ❀ Offer robes, whitewash for stupas, temples, etc., for example, give golden bowls, incense, ointments, and decorations.
- ❀ Feed those who are hungry, or donate to food banks.
- ❀ Delight in abundance, even when you are not experiencing it.
- ❀ Donate clothes, containers, vehicles, and housing.
- ❀ Provide nice places for people to sit and rest.
- ❀ Clean up around Buddhist centers, stupas, etc.
- ❀ Sponsor the building of stupas and temples.
- ❀ Fund the improvement and maintenance of temples and stupas.
- ❀ Financially support your mother and father, monks and nuns, the sick, the old, the feeble—even fools.

Acts of Kindness

- ✋ Care for the Sick
- ✋ Feel genuine empathetic joy when others recover from illnesses.
- ✋ Take care of your parents if they are sick.
- ✋ Help other people when they are ill.
- ✋ Run errands for sick people, delivering medicine and food.
- ✋ Call or visit your parents and show them your appreciation.
- ✋ Attend to your mother and father, monks and nuns, teachers and preceptors, and other advisors.
- ✋ Praise your mother and father.
- ✋ Respect the elders in your family.
- ✋ Praise monastics.
- ✋ Don't look down on people from poor, low-status families.
- ✋ Train in reducing envy.

Don't Steal

- ◈ Don't take money or things that weren't given to you.
- ◈ Prevent other people from being ripped off.
- ◈ Praise former thieves and scammers who have given up their criminal ways.
- ◈ Refrain from taking what was not given.

Empathy and Compassion

- Allow empathy or compassion to arise when you are around those who are helpless.
- Think lovingly and kindly of the sick and senior citizens in your life.
- Prevent the negative acts of others.
- Use careful speech & conflict resolution techniques.
- Quickly reverse thoughts of happiness that may arise when your enemies are ill.
- Apply the teachings to work with emotions such as anger, friction, hypocrisy, jealousy, selfishness, stubbornness, conceit, and envy.
- Rejoice when others get ahead. Mourn their losses.
- When others are praised instead of you, feel that it lifts your boat along with theirs.
- Don't ridicule people for their appearance, age, or status, or those living a pure life.
- Be elevated by the thought of people living a rugged life in poverty, devoted to practice.
- Be uplifted at the thought of privileged people with extremely pure conduct.
- Cheer on and support awesome people who do good deeds.

Work with emotions

Apply the teachings you have received about how to work with emotions.

Conclusion: Living as Though Karma Is Real

Karma means living as if your actions truly matter. Every moment, every interaction, becomes an opportunity to create benefit or harm. This is the essence of ethical training.

Are You Making a Ring of Light?

Our aim as Buddhists is to enact positive deeds continuously, like the ring of light drawn in the dark by a whirling sparkler.

Take a moment to reflect:

- What are some of the recurring habits of goodness in your life?
- Are there ways you might increase their frequency or intensity?
- What would it take to create a life of unrelenting beneficence that glows like that sparkler for the benefit of all?

Evening Review

Before bed, ask yourself:
* Did I do anything today that may cause harm?
* Did I miss an opportunity to help?
* Did I act with integrity, even when no one was watching?

Renew your intention to do even better tomorrow.

Closing Reflection: Who Are You Becoming?

With sustained reflection on karma, you'll change. It's inevitable.

Take a moment now to recognize that shift. What qualities are strengthening in you? What old tendencies are starting to lose their grip?

Some old companions may not resonate with this new direction. But folks who align with the deeper values you're uncovering will start to appear. These will be your people.

Notice that. Trust that. Keep going.

The many karmic roots beneath our life

Chapter 7

Exploration

The Spiritual Friend: A Guiding Light

In Mahayana Buddhism, your personal relationship with a spiritual friend—*a kalyana-mitra*—can deeply shape the entire journey of your practice. Books, teachings, and solo sessions are incredibly valuable, but without someone who sees your unique potential for awakening and helps you untie your inner knots, your practice might stay on the surface. My aim here is to encourage you to seek a connection with someone grounded, kind, wise, and able to guide you in real time.

Reflection: What Would True Support Look Like?

Think about a mentor, teacher, or guide who genuinely helped you grow in an honest, supportive, and transformative way. If you haven't had one, imagine what that connection might feel like.

- ☞ What qualities did they have (or would they have)?
- ☞ What didn't work in past dynamics, or what would you want to avoid?
- ☞ What kind of support would truly help you go deeper in your spiritual unfolding?

Write a few lines on what you personally would really need in a spiritual guide. We'll get to the guru role in Chapter 15.

_____
_____
_____
_____

Cultivating a Spiritual Connection: A Short Field Guide

Here are some qualities to look for when you're considering someone as a potential spiritual friend or guide. Perhaps these touchstones will help your discernment:

Pure Conduct	They uphold the general vows of Buddhist practitioner, the special vows of a Bodhisattva, and the subtle pledges of the Vajrayana beautifully. In other words, they act ethically and consistently, prioritizing non-harm and honesty. Their emphasis is on how they can help you with your practice, not on what you can do for them.
Knowledge	They've studied deeply and truly understand the doctrine according to their lineage, and the teachings of the Buddhadharma in general.
Compassion	They relate with warmth and genuine care, even to difficult people.
Realization	A deep shift was sparked in them by having an experience of the true nature of reality as empty and beyond words and concepts, beyond what our thinking mind can grasp. (This is difficult to determine. So, we rely primarily on their reputation among senior Rinpoches in their lineage, not charisma.)

As you reflect, write down the names of any individuals who come to mind. If none do right now, that's perfectly fine—you can always revisit this as your journey unfolds.

- _____
- _____
- _____
- _____
- _____

Reflection: What would you offer to you teacher or teachers?

When we are cultivating relationship with wiser mentors, sometimes we forget to ask ourselves not only what we hope to get out of it, but how we can help them. Yes, financial offerings are part of it, but also you should know that the ability of someone to teach is dependent on people helping them. In other words, please do help them by volunteering. How do you plan to help?

Conclusion

While the ideal of a personal spiritual friend is a profound aspiration, it can take time to find one. If you haven't yet found a direct guide, continue to connect with the teachings through books, reputable online resources, or local dharma centers. Focus on cultivating the qualities you've identified in a spiritual friend within yourself – integrity, knowledge, compassion, and consistent practice. Keep practicing what you've learned. The very act of engaging sincerely with your ngondro practice, combined with a discerning heart, is often how the right connections begin to manifest. Trust your path, and keep an open mind and heart as you continue your search for the guidance that best supports your unique unfolding.

Chapter 8

Accumulation

Cultivating Merit and Wisdom on the Path

This chapter explores the profound process of accumulation. In the uncommon ngondro, these two accumulations of merit and wisdom work together to foster joy, clear perception, and the mental clarity essential for genuine awakening.

When we intentionally engage in acts that create merit and cultivate wisdom, we're actively transforming our mindstream and creating the inner spaciousness necessary to perceive reality as it truly is.

Accumulating Merit

Merit-making is about cultivating a generous, ethical, patient, joyful, and persevering mindset in our daily lives. Classically, ten activities constitute the basis of merit: giving, virtue, mental development, honouring others, offering service, dedicating merit to others, rejoicing in others' merit, listening to Buddha's teachings, instructing others in the Dharma, and bringing one's own views into accord with the Dharma.

You will notice that your ngondro practice, coupled with your studies and service to your center and spiritual friend or guru, encompasses aspects of all of these. Ngondro makes this all practical and doable in one package. But it does take intentional effort, and something more valuable to us than that. It takes time, ideally every day. As the practice starts to purify emotional turbulence and strengthen your positive inclinations, you will feel it. The wilder you are at the start, the more dramatic the change will be. (By wild, I mean ruled by overwhelming concepts, iron-clad opinions, and emotions.)

Reflections

Start by reflecting on your current relationship with actions that generate positive karmic force:

What types of actions do you perform regularly that generate merit? List at least five positive actions you perform in daily life. Think about simple acts of kindness, generosity, patience, and ethical behaviour.

1.
2.
3.

4.
5.

How often do you consciously engage in acts of virtue, and do you ever feel "burned out" by them? Practice identifying when you feel exhausted or uninspired by your good deeds. What strategies could help you maintain consistent efforts without becoming overwhelmed?

_____
_____
_____
_____

How do you recognize your inner resistance to beneficial practices (like meditation or acts of giving)? Think about times when you've felt resistant to practicing ngondro, doing generous things, or letting go of something pleasurable. How can you gently train yourself to lean into these practices more willingly?

_____
_____

Purifying Emotional Veils

We aren't starting from a neutral place. Our minds are come pre-clouded by what Buddhism calls " afflictions"—unskilful emotional patterns that distort our perception and create suffering. Ngondro systematically helps clear these veils.

Reflection: Emotions and Clarity

When you hear that most emotions are seen as afflictions in Buddhism. How does that strike you?

_____
_____
_____

Where do you notice emotions clouding your clarity most often in your daily life?

_____
_____

Short Exercise: Identifying Your Dominant Emotions Right Now

Check which of these emotional patterns most often clouds your practice or inner peace lately:

- ☐ Anger
- ☐ Desire/Clinging
- ☐ Jealousy/envy
- ☐ Pride/Arrogance

Accumulating Wisdom: Seeing Clearly

The second accumulation involves finding your inherent wisdom that transcends conceptual thinking. Ngondro starts the process of dissolving the cloud-like mental obscuration that prevents direct, unmediated experience of reality.

Reflection

Look at your habitual thought patterns that reinforce a false sense of self. What are these thoughts, and how might meditation help you recognize them as constructs or illusions?

_____
_____
_____
_____
_____

Direct Experience

Go outside or look around the room for a minute. For sixty seconds, try to experience what is there without labelling, judging, or forming concepts about it. Just pure perception. What was that experience like? What did you notice about your mind's tendency to label?

_____
_____
_____

These exercises won't instantly turn you into a Buddha who can see reality as it is. But, do make a few notes about your experience. Years from now, as an accomplished practitioner, you may be amazed at how different your mind is!

Chapter 9

Representation

Your Personal Shrine: A Sacred Space for Practice

Creating a sacred space, whether it's a simple altar or a traditional shrine, can profoundly deepen your practice. It acts as a visual anchor and a constant reminder of your spiritual intentions. A traditional ngondro shrine often includes specific representations of enlightened Body, Speech, and Mind.

Representations of Wisdom:

Body — The Statue

A statue is a visual reminder of awakened embodiment.
Do you already have a statue of the Buddha or a symbolic Buddhist "deity" on your shrine? Would you like it to be filled and consecrated in a traditional manner?

Speech — The Dharma Text

A sacred text, perhaps wrapped in cloth to show respect and keep it clean, represents enlightened speech.
Have you chosen one? If so, what does that text mean to you?

Mind — The Stupa

The stupa symbolizes awakened mind: pure, stable, and all-pervasive.
Do you have a stupa on your shrine? If you want to buy one (made of metal, stone, or clear acrylic), you might show it to a leader at your Dharma center and ask what traditional items—such as a mantra scroll, small relic, or powdered incense—could be added to its interior.
If a stupa isn't accessible or desired, you can substitute another representation of awakened mind, such as a Vajrayana implement like a *phurba* or *driguk*.

Driguk

If you can't afford specific items, it is still possible to acquire traditional items. Some practitioners, especially elders, have adopted a simpler style of practice and may have extra ritual items they no longer need and would be happy to give to you. It's often worth asking around at a Dharma center when you are gathered there with other practitioners.

Phurba

Offerings: Cultivating Generosity and Connection

Offerings are a powerful way to train the mind to give without grasping and to create the conditions for spiritual abundance.

Morning Water Bowl Offering Practice

What You'd Need:

- 7 or 8 small bowls (metal, glass, or ceramic)
- A water pitcher or measuring cup
- A surface or tray to place them on
- A sink, a sponge, and a cloth to clean and dry your bowls.

Visualize and Practice: As you fill each bowl from left to right, imagine offering the pure water, as you pour, to the buddhas and bodhisattvas. You might ask for a traditional water offering verse at your center and recite it as you pour. Let this become a meditation in itself.

In the morning, fill the bowls mindfully. In the evening, pour the water outside, clean and dry the bowls, and then either turn them over or lean them gently against each other to finish drying.

Okay, so I've implied something you "should" do. How do you feel about that? Happy to have a regimen to follow? Rebellious, because you resent being told what to do or can't stand religious dogma? I view you as an empowered adult: your level of enthusiasm for the more religious aspects of Tibetan Buddhism is not a big deal.

Feelings: Who Cares?

There is a reason why I've been asking probing questions about how you feel. Questions that are never asked by Tibetan lamas. It's because I've been around the block a few times and met some people who, outwardly at least, seemed unchanged by decades of practice. One thing they seem to have in common is that they come off as oblivious to their own feelings, especially those that are socially unacceptable.

Having noticed this, I make a point of identifying my emotions. I even go so far as to say my difficult-to-acknowledge feelings aloud.

For example, this very morning, I noted how incredibly bored I am by the work of final polishing of this workbook. Repetitive detail work with little novelty is really hard for this ADHD elder to complete. Stating that allows me to examine what boredom is emotionally. Bored is just a label. It feels like anguish in my chest. Having identified the anguish in my chest, I can liberate it with the techniques of Dzogchen. (I have an affinity with the Dzogchen approach)

I'm not heavy-handed about it, constantly searching for emotions as if they were problems to be solved. However, I am not tuned out, numbed out, or in denial about my emotions either.

I recommend that approach.

Closing Prompt: Your Shrine as a Mirror

Take a moment to sit in front of your shrine. Light a candle or a stick of incense. Gaze at the three symbols—body, speech, and mind—and your offerings.

Ask yourself:

How does gazing at this shrine feel compared to looking at ordinary things like a city street of a cell phone?

What intention do I want to strengthen each time I see it?

Write that intention in a sentence below. If you like, tuck it under your statue as a hidden offering.

_____
_____
_____
_____
_____
_____

Chapter 10

Interconnection

Practicing with Body, Speech, and Mind

In most spiritual paths, you'll find practices focusing on the body, others on the voice, and still others on the mind. In Tibetan Buddhism, we intentionally weave them together to transform the whole person.

When you engage in a full ngondro session, you are:
- Moving your body: through prostrations or bowing.
- Using your voice: by reciting mantras and verses.
- Visualizing and contemplating: working with your imagination and inner awareness.
- By doing so, you're cleaning up patterns that no longer serve you.

Embodied Practice: Why Every Part of You Matters

Body Practice: Prostrations as Liberation

Lama Tharchin Rinpoche used to tell us that churning the intellectual mind and expecting enlightenment was like churning water and hoping to get butter.

You can't think your way to awakening. You have to move out of old habits, out of ego, and into pure presence.

Prostrations are far more than a religious formality. When done with intention, they become a profound embodied act of purification and humility. You bow to acknowledge that there is something immensely valuable worth bowing to—the awakened potential in others, in yourself, and in the path itself.

The Threefold Purpose of Prostrations:

Purification of Karma: Prostrations help you shift out of default physical patterns and plant new, wholesome imprints through a gesture of respect and reverence.

Cultivating Humility and Receptivity: Bowing softens self-importance and helps the heart open.

Physical Fitness: It provides balance to long periods of sitting.

Your Relationship with Prostrations

Ask yourself:
How do you feel about prostrating?
Does it come naturally or feel awkward?
Write a short reflection on what comes up when you imagine or do a full-body prostration. Be honest.

_____
_____
_____
_____
_____

Learning Full-Body Prostration

There are many ways to learn the physical technique. If you're new, I encourage you to search for a video online. What matters most is your intention.

When you bow:

Touch your joined hands to your head (representing buddha form), throat (buddha speech), and heart (buddha mind), then reach down and put your palms on the floor,

Slide your body fully to the ground. Rise slowly, returning to standing erect, and bring your joined hands to your head, throat and heart. Repeat.

Try three prostrations initially. Gradually increase your count. Eventually, most people will be able to do 108 in ten to fifteen minutes.

Speech Practice: Clearing the Way with Your Voice

In Tibetan Buddhism, we don't just think the teachings; we say them. We sing them. We let them pass through our vocal cords and ride out on our breath.

The spoken word is profoundly powerful. In Vajrayana, that power is actively harnessed. Every syllable recited aloud becomes part of the work of transformation.

When you speak your practice text, it:

- ★ Reinforces your intention.
- ★ Anchors your wandering mind.
- ★ Engages your breath and subtle energy.

Reflection Prompt: Your Relationship with Sacred Speech

Take a moment to reflect on these questions:

Have you ever spoken or sung a prayer, poem, or chanted aloud before? Do you feel self-conscious when you vocalize spiritual words?

Mind Practice: Clearing the Way with Visualization

Visualization in Tibetan Buddhism is a practice that uses the mind's innate creativity to rewire how you perceive yourself and the world. You are not tripping out to escape reality; you are practicing seeing things as they truly are.

And what you see—light bodies, vast fields of refuge, awakened faces gazing back at you—is a vivid mirror of what's possible when you go beyond the limits of your current operating system that we might call human psychology.

In ngondro, the visualized buddhas are symbolic, vivid mirrors of your own enlightened potential, refined and radiant. You may picture Guru Rinpoche, the perfect master who brings all teachings into one path. Or Vajradhara, dark blue, the essence of buddhahood itself. They are not fantasy. They are like artist renditions of how your mind looks when it's free.

The Three Purposes of Visualization in ngondro:

- ◇ Mental Engagement: Visualization brings your whole attention online, focusing the mind.
- ◇ Habit Reversal: It helps cut through deep, ingrained assumptions about identity and reality.
- ◇ Familiarization: You become intimately familiar with awakening in an inspiring symbolic form.

What Does Light Mean to You?

In Vajrayana visualization, "deities," awakened forms are made of light—translucent, radiant, insubstantial.

What images or metaphors does light bring to mind for you?

How might it affect your consciousness if you regarded yourself as composed only of light?

Mini Practice: First Glimpses

Sit quietly and breathe. Choose one form: Guru Rinpoche or Vajradhara. Place them above your head or in front of you, slightly elevated. Don't worry it is not perfect. Imagine a body made of radiant light, seated in meditation, with a peaceful gaze and infinite kindness. Let your breath pass through you slowly as you picture them. Gaze with eyes open, softly, downward or ahead. When needed, briefly close your eyes to refresh the image. Hold the image for a few moments. Then let it dissolve into light and rest.

Adapting Your Practice (If Visualization is Tough)

Perfectionism can whisper that your visualization should be better, more precise. Ngondro visualization isn't about *avoiding* your inner experience of 'samsara' by focusing on a sacred appearance. You don't need to create a Pixar-perfect mental image. That appearance might be clear as day, or more like sensing a presence just outside your field of view. Either will fulfill its function.

If vivid visualization feels challenging, try one or more of the following alternatives.
- 📖 Use a printed image or thangka during practice as your visual aid.
- 📖 Focus on the words and meaning of the practice rather than the visual aspect.
- 📖 Sing the verses with full feeling and feel it in your body.

Conclusion: Your Integrated Path

Vajrayana Buddhism is characterized by having very many different forms of practice. That makes it possible for more people with different strengths to have effective practice sessions.

What areas are strong for you?

Some examples:

I am very sincere
I respect the tradition I am practicing in.
I have faith in my own capacity to awaken
I have time in my day for practice
I enjoy my singing and chanting voice
I learn foreign languages easily.
I can sit on a meditation cushion for up to two hours in one sitting.
I have lots of afflictive emotions to use as fuel for my practice.
I can visualize things in my minds-eye easily.
I have access to good lamas
I am diligent in practice
I'm okay with solitude
I'm really interested in this.

Affirmations for this chapter:

"I will show up on my cushion just as I am, bringing every part of me into my practice."
"I'm no different than any other practitioner, strong in some areas and weak in others."

Chapter 11

Protection

Going for Refuge

Going for refuge marks a profound step in the life of a dharma practitioner. It's when we consciously choose to place our trust and protection in the Three Jewels: the Buddha, the Dharma, and the Sangha. This act of refuge is means making an ongoing commitment to turn toward them as our guide star, guiding us through life's inevitable challenges.

In this chapter, we'll explore various exercises designed to help you deepen your connection with the Three Jewels, learn the deeper meanings they represent, and integrate the practice of refuge into your daily life.

Reflecting on the Three Jewels

Take a few moments to reflect on the following:

Buddha: What does the figure of the Buddha represent for you personally? How does the Buddha's example inspire you to overcome obstacles and cultivate wisdom?
Dharma: What teachings or practices resonate most deeply with you on your path? How do these teachings help clarify your understanding of suffering and its cessation?
Sangha: When you hear the word sangha, who comes to mind? An exalted monastic from far away? Your friends in your online or in-person community?

Write about how the Buddha, Dharma, and Sangha can act as your personal "North Star." In what ways have you already experienced their guidance in your life?

_____
_____
_____
_____
_____
_____

What do you think is meant by the words "refuge" and "protection" here?

_____
_____

Meditation on the Refuge Tree

Visualizing whatever Vajrayana deity is chief in your ngondro text, as a symbolic representation of your latent qualities of awakening, can help bring the practice of refuge to life.

Close your eyes and imagine a vast, luminous refuge tree, with the central deity seated at its center. Surrounding him are all the buddhas, bodhisattvas, and enlightened beings of the lineage. Feel their presence as your refuge.

Imagine yourself as part of this vast spiritual field, standing in awe before the refuge tree. See the infinite beings—your loved ones, acquaintances, and even your enemies—all around you. Imagine them all bowing down with you in reverence to awakened mind.

Write about your experience. What feelings arose when you imagined yourself there?

_____
_____
_____
_____
_____
_____
_____
_____
_____
_____

Contemplating the Refuge Vow

The refuge vow is a powerful commitment to spiritual awakening. Reflect on the following: What does taking the refuge vow mean to you?

Journal your thoughts on the refuge vow, and consider what might hold you back from fully committing to it. (Even if you haven't taken part in a refuge ceremony).

_____
_____
_____
_____

How does turning to the Three Jewels help you make decisions in everyday ethical dilemmas?

___
___
___
___
___

Doubts

Emotional upheavals or sudden changes in circumstances can turn your mind negative at times. Suddenly, it seems as though everyone is against you. You may even doubt the three jewels. At those times, it is like a tornado has come into your life and turned everything upside down. I suggest refraining from making decisions you will later regret at those times. Consider refraining from talking to or texting the people involved immediately.

Often, there is a physical health issue that is subtly affecting your mind. Please rest and take care of your physical health during those times. Eat healthy, grounding, nutritious food. You can suspend your practice for a while during a crisis and resume it when you feel better and everything doesn't seem so bleak and hopeless.

Coping with feeling isolated:

How can the sangha (even if unseen or online) provide support when practicing solo? How does the concept of the "refuge tree" address that feeling of being alone on the path?

___
___
___
___
___

Conclusion: Reaffirming Your Refuge

As you continue your practice of refuge, remember that it is not a one-time act but an ongoing commitment to align your actions with the wisdom and compassion of the Three Jewels. Each time you go for refuge, you strengthen your intention to seek liberation from suffering and cultivate the path of awakening.

Chapter 12

Motivation

Cultivating Bodhicitta

Anyone at any time can decide to stop categorizing beings according to whether they are more or less deserving of compassion.

The cultivation of bodhicitta in the ngondro can seem straightforward at first glance. You recite your bodhisattva vow 100,000 times while visualizing all sentient beings and the refuge tree, with some additional recitations to ensure thoroughness. While reciting, you can contemplate the four boundless states, and after finishing your recitation, you briefly practice tonglen. In some ngondro traditions, the bodhicitta verse is accumulated in conjunction with refuge. In any case, our vow is to awaken so that we can bring others to that state as well.

This practice draws deeply from the vast world of Mahayana Buddhism. For many, especially lay practitioners, comprehensive sutra-level studies might not be a primary focus. This was certainly true for me. This chapter, in the main, aims to touch on core Mahayana topics lightly, introducing essential vocabulary you'll need as a practitioner, even if your main focus is on practice over philosophy.

It can be tempting to skip over Sanskrit and Tibetan words if you don't enjoy foreign languages. However, these terms are fundamental and will likely reappear throughout your practice journey until you become familiar with them. They are beautiful words, dripping with love and compassion. They forge a link between ourselves and the greats of the past who perfectly embodied bodhicitta.

Key Mahayana Terms: A Quick Reference

These Sanskrit terms are vital to understanding the Mahayana path. Draw a line between each term, below, and its short definition:

Anuttara samyak-sambodhi	Compassion
Dharani	Enjoyment body
Karuna	Emptiness
Nirmanakaya	The wisdom of a Buddha (Mahayana def)
Sambhogakaya	Buddha nature
Dharmakaya	Discourse
Shastra	Unsurpassed complete awakening
Shunyata	Buddhist incantations with a purpose
Jnana	All Buddhas' realization of the true nature of reality
Svabhavikakaya	The inseparability of the three kayas
Tathagatagarbha	Manifest body of awakening

Common Pitfalls

Thinking about bodhicitta and bodhisattvas often feels inherently good, and it can be tempting to stop there. But "thinking about" is often a conceptual, sometimes non-committal approach. Here are some questions to ask yourself to ensure your Bodhicitta practice remains wholehearted and genuinely transformative.

Reflection: Am I Soothing Myself Instead of Transforming?

It's tempting to use compassion teachings as a way to comfort myself and feel better. However, true bodhicitta calls for deeper engagement. Ask yourself — am I developing a personal long-term commitment or simply lolling in an ocean of love as a form of self-comforting?

Reflection: Am I Keeping It on the Cushion?

Bodhicitta practice extends beyond the meditation cushion. Reflect — does my vow to cultivate compassion show up in my daily life? Am I truly acting with bodhicitta when I engage with others? Do I curb hidden agendas and do my best to help the people around me altruistically?

Reflection: Am I practicing passive-aggression in disguise?

Do I notice any hidden bitterness in myself that might subtly leak out in my interactions with others? Am I honest with myself about unfinished emotional business that may affect my actions? Am I learning new, honest yet non-aggressive ways to work with conflict?

The Buddhafield: A Vision of Awakening

In Mahayana Buddhism, fully awakened buddhas and great bodhisattvas abide in realms called pure lands or buddhafields. These are not ordinary places; they exist beyond our usual experience of space and time, immaculate abodes created through pure wisdom and compassion.

Even though we cannot perceive them with our ordinary senses, high-level bodhisattvas can. From their pure lands, they send forth emanations to help all of us who are deeply engaged in samsara. They offer teachings, protection, healing, and inspiration, meeting us in whatever form we can most easily recognize and trust.

While we might think of these as latent aspects of our own consciousness, many devotional practitioners approach this literally, and in my experience, their practice often flourishes remarkably based on faith and devotion.

When you imagine a buddhafield, think about a place free of harm, fear, or confusion. A place where every detail—the trees, rivers, birds, and mountains—reflects the awakened qualities of compassion, clarity, and peace.

Practicing the Four Boundless Qualities

In Mahayana Buddhism, our hearts must expand beyond the narrow circle of "me and mine" to embrace all life. The Four Boundless States (AKA the Four Immeasurables)—equanimity, love, compassion, and joy—train us to meet the world with a boundless mind. On any given day, you can focus on one, a pair, or all four, while accumulating recitations of your ngondro's bodhicitta verse.

Do you find you can simultaneously recite, count, and practice the Four Boundless States? The most challenging aspect of the practice may be developing a sense of equal concern for all living beings. When you think about it, this is a very radical notion. Why do you think Buddhism has that value when other religions may be more partial? How might that relate to your future awakening?

Journaling Prompts: Mahayana and Bodhicitta

These prompts encourage deeper reflection on the concepts introduced in this chapter.

Your Turning Point: Was there a moment or insight that made you want your spiritual practice to be about helping others, not just finding personal peace? Describe that moment (or your current feeling about it) in a few sentences.

_____
_____
_____
_____
_____
_____
_____
_____

Equanimity Check-In & Real-World Conflicts:

Choose three people: one you love, one you feel neutral toward, and one you have difficulty with. For each, write a sentence about what it would mean to extend equal goodwill toward them.

Recall a recent personal or political situation that stirred up anger, fear, or disgust. If you had approached it with true equanimity, how might your thoughts, speech, or actions have shifted?

Personal Barriers to Boundless Love: Reflect honestly: Are there certain types of people, groups, or even specific individuals that you find it challenging to extend loving-kindness toward? Why do you think these barriers exist? How might Buddhist practice help you loosen these knots?

Navigating pain and joy in practice: Bodhicitta practice doesn't always make us feel good — sometimes it exposes pain, sorrow, or our own limitations. Reflect on a time when spiritual practice was painful but ultimately fruitful for you. How might discomfort be a sign of genuine growth?

Conclusion: Strengthening the Foundation

Cultivating bodhicitta is the very foundation for every step on the path to awakening. It requires deliberate training, both in extending compassion to all beings and in recognizing the illusory nature of self and other. By returning to these practices daily, we stabilize our intention and prepare for more profound realization.

Chapter 13

Purification

Vajrasattva Practice: Clearing Karmic Repercussions

Vajrasattva practice is the central method in Tibetan Buddhism for purifying the negative karma that can cloud our minds and weigh down our future, before it ripens. While early Buddhism teaches that we can improve our circumstances by reflecting on our mistakes, feeling genuine remorse, and making amends, Vajrayana offers a more powerful approach: purification.

Through the heartfelt recitation of Vajrasattva's Hundred-Syllable Mantra, we can dissolve the destructive patterns of past actions—even those that could otherwise lead to great suffering. Vajrasattva practice works by invoking our deep potential for awakening and clearing the stains that obscure it.

Effective purification relies on four key powers: sincere regret, the descending nectar, a strong resolve to change, and the recitation of the mantra itself. If practiced fully, Vajrasattva can clear even the heaviest karmic imprints and protect our health, vitality, and future path.

Workbook Exercise: Understanding Vajrasattva Practice

Reflect and Respond

Vajrasattva Visualization: Imagine the beautiful white sambhogakaya buddha, Vajrasattva, seated above your head. Feel him radiating purity and peace.

Symbolism Reflection

Vajrasattva may appear alone or in union with Vajratopa. Both images symbolize ultimate purity and the inseparability of wisdom and compassion. Reflect on your reaction to this imagery. Does it feel foreign, natural, inspiring, confusing?

_____
_____
_____
_____
_____

Journal Prompts:

Reflect on your emotional history with the idea of "purification." Were you raised in a religious or cultural setting that made you feel as though your very essence was impure? How might ideas about Vajrayana purification be different from that old conditioning?

_____
_____
_____
_____

Somatic Reflection: Feeling the Hundred-Syllable Mantra in the Body

Sit in front of your shrine in your practice space. Hold your mala. Relax your body without slumping. As you quietly recite the Hundred-Syllable Mantra at a slow and steady pace, pay close attention to the physical sensations that arise.

During recitation, notice:

Where in your body you feel vibration from your voice.
How your breathing changes (Is it shallow? Deep? Strained? Relaxed?).
Any tension or tightness in your jaw, shoulders, throat, or chest.
Whether your posture feels steady or unsettled.
Any other sensations.
Shifts in mental chatter or emotional tone.

After Recitation, Journal Briefly:
What physical sensations did you notice most strongly while reciting?

_____
_____

Were there moments where the mantra and your in-breath and out-breath felt comfortable because they were naturally synchronized?

_____
_____

How could you recitation become more relaxed, natural, and aligned with your breathing?

_____

_____

When you were finished with your recitation, did you feel different?

_____

In truth, you are Vajrasattva already—your core is present, clear, wakefulness. Sit silently like that, beautiful and radiant—in your translucent light body.

Chapter 14

Multiplication

The practice of mandala offering can be a very enjoyable experience. Who knew that absorbing yourself in offering up everything you love could be a happy thing? At the same time, if you haven't started your mandala offering accumulation yet, the thought can be daunting. I know that it can seem physically complicated. The visualizations are entirely new to you. The concepts are complex and foreign. There are many helpful pointers in my book, so please re-read that chapter before starting. You will succeed at this, quickly getting the hang of the practice.

I have found that the two most helpful things when you are starting out are in-person demonstration of how to do the practice and owning the proper equipment.

Modeling

Watching the videos of people doing mandala offerings on YouTube is helpful. Remember that there are varied styles of making the physical offerings in different lineages. If you are watching monks in a monastery, remember that they are young men. The ideal form they demonstrate —sitting cross-legged on the floor for hours, holding the pan high with perfect posture —is something to strive for if you can. But you will need to adapt if you have disabilities. Don't let your mind make you feel like a loser! The point is to make a big effort. How that will look will vary.

That's why I recommend practicing with experienced lay practitioners in the same room. In an instant, so much will be clarified.

Remember the Purpose

Keep in mind that this is a structured method for creating vast positive karmic force (merit) while dismantling attachment and dualistic thinking. It draws together three essential aspects: the imagination (mental offering), the voice (reciting the offering verse), and the body (physically offering). Together, they forge momentum on the path to awakening. In the future, you will have accumulated the vast reservoirs of merit necessary to achieve buddhahood. You will meet more teachers, receive teachings, and realize your true nature.

In a more profound sense, offering everything to the buddhas and the bodhisattvas will train you to move beyond ordinary concepts of transactional giving. Through continuous, open-hearted offering, you will touch the purity that has always been present within you.

Merit-making is like planting a seed.

Equipment

Recently, I had a ngondro retreat in my shrine room here in rural California. I was shocked to see how extra-hard people were working to compensate for a sub-standard mandala pan. You do not want a flat mandala offering pan! It needs to be slightly domed. Don't buy an undersized pan. You want it to be at least 6.5 inches in diameter. Copper or brass. Also, manufacturers and stores want to charge more, so they will put raised ornaments on the sides of the pan to increase the purchase price. That will just make it more difficult to handle. Get a plain one if you can. If you are in the U.S., I recommend Namse Bangso, the bookstore of KTC monastery in New York. You will be taking a big risk from Amazon, Ebay or Walmart for this particular item. The same goes for your accomplishment mandala.

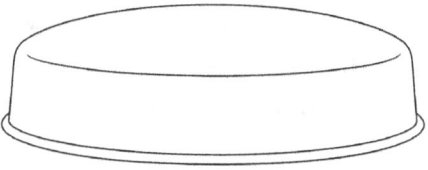

Mandala offering pan

You can use saffron rice. I even gave you instructions for how to make it in the book. If you can afford it, though, tiny tumbled semi-precious stones will be more pleasant. Rice doesn't feel as nice, and can get sticky if you sweat. For this, you can buy the stones anywhere. I use eBay or local rock shops. Tiny tumbled amethyst, jasper, etc, will do. It is fun to pick out your own.

Exercise: Setting Up Your Accomplishment Mandala

Connect your mind, body, and voice with the act of pure offering.

Step 1: Choose your materials.

If you have a tiered mandala set for the Accomplishment Mandala: Set it up on your shrine according to your lama or group's procedure, filling it with clean rice, saffron rice, or semi-precious stones. If you can't get that information, just fill each tier with your substance and place the top ornament.

Or, you can use a clean, flat dish (like a small plate) and a handful of clean dry rice or five piles if that is the custom your lama follows.

Or you can imagine it there in front of you.

Step 2: Prepare your mind.

Recall your refuge sources—your teachers, lineage figures, and buddhas while preparing your accomplishment mandala and placing it on the shrine.

Bring to mind your wish to offer the entire universe to them as an act of pure offering.

The Mandala Universe and the Art of Offering

The visualizations in the mandala offering practice are gigantic, and it's natural to feel overwhelmed. To help you expand your imagination, I'll offer some traditional classifications of offerings. While there are no rigid rules for how you *must* do this, the point is to offer relentlessly—these categories can provide a helpful framework to spark your imagination and ensure thoroughness.

In my case, I would find myself running out of ideas of things to offer, so I was happy to incorporate all of these four classifications of offerings. I found that knowing these came in a little bit handy for me later on.

Visualizing the Outer Offering

Familiarize Yourself

Look up an image of the Buddhist cosmological world: Mount Meru, the four continents, the subcontinents, the sun, the moon, the heavens above, and the hells below.
(Use the term "Buddhist Cosmology Mount Meru" in an image search.) Examine it.

Expand Your Offering

Multiply this 'world' in your imagination:
1,000 worlds equals one first-order universe.
1,000 first-order universes equals one second-order universe.
1,000 second-order universes equals a trichiliocosm.
Now, imagine offering the entire trichiliocosm to the refuge sources!

The Sixteen Offering Goddesses

Now visualize sixteen graceful offering goddesses, each presenting pleasing offerings of sound, touch, scent, beauty, music, respectively, to your refuge deities.

Inner Offerings

Offer Your Body and Mind

Picture your body laid out symbolically:

- ◎ Your trunk is Mount Meru.
- ◎ Your arms and legs are the four continents.
- ◎ Your eyes are the sun and moon.

Offer the Intangibles

Offer your senses, thoughts, memories, karmic seeds — past, present, and future.

Secret Offerings

Imagine pure visions of luminous spheres, infinite buddhas, rainbow light fields — the visions you will encounter someday.

Working with Your Pan

Hold the pan in your hand, open side down. In order to remember the implicit directionality, imagine the surface as a flat world. (Your actual physical location and compass directions do not matter here.) In certain lineages, such as Patrul Rinpoche's, the far side is west, but generally the practitioner is assumed to be facing east. Check with your spiritual friend.

Memorize the directions, for example:

Far side = East
Right = South
Near side = West
Left = North
Center = Mount Meru

If you haven't done the practice before, place seven small piles of offerings in this order (Start by placing a pile representing Mt. Meru on the center point of the pan and then go clockwise, starting with the far side), while saying the names of Mount Meru, the four continents, and the sun and moon out loud.

Center (Mount Meru)
East (Purvavideha)
South (Jambudvipa)
West (Aparagodaniya)
North (Uttarakuru)
East (Sun)
West (Moon)

Now you can pour the offering substances into your container if you haven't started accumulating yet. If you have, keep going.

Reflection: Merging the Traditional with the Contemporary

How do you feel about the idea of offering everything you love — your home, your favorite foods, the people and animals you cherish — even if only in imagination? Write honestly about any resistance, skepticism, or enthusiasm you notice.

_____
_____
_____
_____

Experiential Shift:

After attempting a session of mandala offerings (even just mentally without a pan), did you notice any change in your mental, emotional state, or how your body feels?

_____
_____
_____

Inner Dialogue Exercise: Giving It All Away

Take a moment for a conversation with yourself. Ask yourself these questions and jot down what comes up.
"What do I love most in this life?"
(Pause. Let images arise: people, places, objects, pets, nature, sensations, dreams.)

_____
_____
_____
_____
_____

"Am I willing to mentally offer this as well?"

_____
_____
_____
_____
_____

"What else have I longed for, or chased after?"

_____
_____
_____

"Can I place them in the offering, without holding back?"
(Imagine placing each one, lovingly, into a luminous pile.)

_____
_____

"If I let it all go, what remains?"

_____

_____

At the end of your practice, imagine the offering, the offeror, and the recipient into light and then into you. Rest in that unity.

Chapter 15

Unification

Guru Yoga: Connecting with Awakened Mind

Guru Yoga taps into our natural respect, admiration, and trust for an extraordinary teacher, blending devotion and imagination to reveal our hidden potential for awakening. You may not have a guru yet. Take your time with that. In that case, work with the symbolic guru figure in your ngondro as it is.

This chapter will show you how to approach Guru Yoga practice with clarity, heart, and good sense.

Understanding the Teacher-Student Relationship

Reflection: Recognizing Positive Influence

Think of someone in your life—past or present—who influenced your character for the better.

What was it about their way of being, not just their words, that affected you?

How did you feel in their presence?

What did you start to see differently after being around them?

Journal briefly on whether that person functioned, even unofficially, like a spiritual teacher might.

_____
_____
_____
_____
_____
_____
_____

Inner Dialogue Exercise: The Skeptic and the Seeker

Write a short inner conversation between two voices within you: one skeptical of needing a guru, and one open to the possibility.

Let the Skeptic ask hard questions about *authority*, *projection*, or *past letdowns*.

Let the Seeker respond sincerely, drawing from your aspirations for awakening and your own felt experience of trust, reverence, or inspiration. Let them go back and forth until the conversation feels complete.

_____
_____
_____
_____
_____
_____
_____
_____
_____

Contemplative Question: Who Could You Trust to Guide You Deeply?

Imagine a guru who:
- Believes in your innate goodness.
- Has trained in wisdom and compassion for decades.
- Sees your potential more clearly than you do.

Ask yourself:
Would you be willing to follow that person's guidance?
What would you need to see in them to entrust them with that role?

_____
_____
_____
_____

Discernment: Identifying a Qualified Teacher

Dialogue Practice: The Friend Who Doesn't Know

Imagine your skeptical friend asks you, "Why would you consider having a guru in the first place? Aren't you afraid of being controlled?" Write a response as though you were talking to this friend. Keep your tone non-defensive, grounded, and honest. Use your own reasons, doubts, and hopes.

Case Study: Vetting Online Dharma Access

Examine an inspiring Dharma teacher whose videos, books, or articles you have read or whom you have listened to online over time. Research:
- Their lineage and background.
- Who their teachers were.
- Whether they offer empowerments or retreats in person in a place you can get to.
- Will in-person and online classes be financially accessible for you?
- How will you assess what their conduct is like offline?

Guided Journaling: Early Signs

Spend a week following the practice instructions from a qualified teacher you are curious about. At the end of the week, journal your observations:
How did the practices affect your emotional state, habits, and perspective?
Do you feel more open, relaxed, and clear?

Long-View Visualization: The Ideal Relationship

Visualize being twenty years further into your spiritual path. You've found a trustworthy guide and have studied and practiced closely for decades. In a paragraph or two, describe:
- How does this long-term relationship feel?
- What kind of practitioner have you become?
- What has remained challenging?

Understanding The Four Kinds of Qualified Vajrayana Teachers

Quiz: Recognizing Qualified Vajrayana Teachers

Draw a line to match each description below to the correct traditional category on the left:

Tulku	Someone who has come to be regarded by the community as a lama, despite a lack of formal education in a religious academy or supervised long-term retreat because of their qualities and self-education.
Scholar	Someone who has completed years in supervised, cloistered retreats, accomplishing the lineage practices. Authorized to teach them by a lineage-holder.
Yogi or Yogini	A person who has accomplished years in a Buddhist scholastic academy and years in cloistered supervised retreat, and may or may not also be recognized as a tulku.
Community-arisen lama	Has spent eight to twenty years training in a monastic academy and was given the title Khenpo, Khenmo, Geshe, or Geshema.
King-like Lama	Someone who was recognized as the rebirth of a great lama of the past, and trained from childhood to hold their lineage accordingly.

Approaching Guru Yoga Practice

An Image of Your Guru

If you haven't found your guru yet, draw a picture. Grab a pencil, sit down, and set aside all thoughts about what you should draw. If you find that using your dominant hand stimulates many contrived thoughts, "They have to be like this or that," use your other hand and just let go. See what appears when you put it on paper.

Your Guru

If this first drawing didn't come together for you, no problem. Grab some more paper and draw like a wild thing, from your heart's interior, with the intention that symbolic clues will emerge.

A still more uncontrived image of your Guru

Taking the Result as the Path: Visualizing Yourself as Awakened

Most guru yoga practices begin with envisioning yourself as a wisdom deity, composed of light – a key principle of Vajrayana known as "taking the result as the path."

Reflection: Seeing Yourself Differently

What comes up for you when you imagine yourself already awakened—with a body made of light, a mind of pure wisdom, and your speech as mantra? Write a little about that.

_____
_____
_____
_____

Self-Check: Readiness for the Vajrayana Approach
In a few sentences, assess your comfort with the idea of "taking the result as the path"—acting and thinking as if you are already a buddha. Does this feel motivating? Intimidating? Unbelievable?

_____
_____
_____
_____

Empowerment Visualization Mapping
On the diagram below, draw a simple outline of a body. Mark the forehead, throat, heart, and navel. Next to each, write the corresponding syllable (OM, AH, HUNG, HRIH) and color (white, red, blue, green).

A practitioner imagines receiving the four empowerments from his spiritual mentor.

Resting in the Nature of Mind: After visualizing the four lights and imagining yourself merging with the guru figure in light, sit quietly until persistent thoughts intrude. No effort, no visualizing.

What was the flavor or texture of that rest, in your own words?

_____
_____
_____

Integrating Guru Yoga into Daily Life

A New Habit of Mind

Go about your day integrated with the guru. Your body is made of light, your words are mantra, and your mind is buddha-mind

Alternatively, go about your day as though you are circumambulating the guru figure—in the form of the symbolic deity—on your right, elevated at the level of your shoulder. Mentally recite the guru yoga mantra in your text. Your world and everything in it is the pure land of that Awakened One.

Closing Journal

Is there a way you are currently "at war" with others, yourself, or the world? How might deep guru yoga practice soften that pattern?

_____
_____
_____
_____
_____
_____

Chapter 16

Integrating Ngondro into Your Life

This chapter provides exercises and reflections designed to help you seamlessly integrate your ngondro practice into the fabric of your daily life.

Workbook Exercises: Integrating ngondro into Your Life

Reflection: Identifying Strengths and Advantages

We each have personal habits of underestimating or overestimating ourselves. If you are on the under-estimation track, here are some ideas about how to look for the qualities in you that can make you a good ngondro practitioner. You:

Love the imagery
Feel "on fire" with motivation
Feel close to a guru or lineage
Look forward to getting fit from prostrations
Feel humble
Have good relations with the sangha
Have a supportive home situation
Love the beauty of the words of the text
Have okay health
Are naturally compassionate
Have time in your day for practice
Are smart enough to understand the practice

Reflection: Identifying Obstacles

Are there obstacles coming up for you about ngondro practice? Take a moment to pinpoint what feels daunting. Consider the common challenges below, or identify your own:

Psychological blocks: Inner resistance or doubts.
Health or fitness issues: Physical limitations that might impact practice.
Lack of private space: Difficulty finding a quiet, dedicated area.
Caregiving responsibilities: Time constraints due to family commitments.
Issues with your childhood religion: Lingering discomfort or conflict.
Being drunk or high frequently: Barriers to focus, consistency, and good conduct.
Lack of motivation: Difficulty finding the drive to start or continue.

Lack of peer support: Feeling isolated in your practice.
Lack of a reliable personal spiritual mentor: Uncertainty about guidance.
Conflicts at the dharma center: Interpersonal issues that cause distraction.
Imagery or words of the ngondro text: Discomfort with specific elements.
Spouse or family opposition: Resistance from loved ones.

If these common issues are coming up for you, don't be embarrassed to talk to a spiritual friend about them. You are not alone.

Writing a Ngondro Vision Statement

Craft a short paragraph describing your aspirations for your ngondro practice. Start with: "I am choosing to do the ngondro because..."
You might consider including:

- The transformation you hope to experience.
- The kind of practitioner you aspire to become.
- How you wish to benefit others through your practice now and in the future.

_____
_____
_____
_____
_____
_____
_____
_____
_____
_____

Clarify Your Ngondro Path: Essential Questions for Your Center or Teacher

Use this section as a practical guide. These are crucial questions every practitioner should ask their teacher or center coordinator before formally beginning ngondro.

Transmission & Empowerments

- Have I received the text reading transmission (lung) for the ngondro text?
- Is empowerment required for the entire ngondro, for specific sections (e.g., Vajrasattva), or is it not required?
- If empowerment is required, how often is it offered?
- Can I begin now and attend empowerments later?

Group Practice & Support

- Is there a group ngondro session I can attend (online or in-person)?
- Are senior students available for occasional guidance?
- Am I encouraged to check in with a mentor regularly?

Accumulation Guidelines

- What are the required accumulation numbers in this lineage?
- Can practices be done sequentially or concurrently?
- Is there flexibility in how many I must complete for each section?
- What is the proper way to count? (e.g., use of mala, clickers, tally sheets)

Session Format & Flexibility

- Am I required to complete the full text each session?
- Can I split a session across different parts of the day?
- Is any off-the-cushion accumulation allowed?

Physical Accommodations

- What can I do if I'm physically unable to perform full prostrations?
- Are there approved alternative practices for disability or illness?
- Do I physically struggle with one of the five accumulations?
- Can I discuss a personal issue privately with my guru?

Planning Your Ngondro Life: A Practical Reflection

Your Time Plan

On average, how many minutes a day can you realistically dedicate to ngondro? Do you want to approach your practice with a specific future completion date in mind or in a more relaxed way?

| 20 | 40 | 60 | 80 | 100 | 120 |
| 30 | 50 | 70 | 90 | 110 | 120 |

Circle the number of minutes a day you can commit to.

What part of the day works best for you?

Can you adjust your daily rhythm (wake time, work schedule, screen time) to support consistent practice?

Write your ideal ngondro practice schedule here:

_____
_____
_____
_____
_____

Perfectionism Check-In

True or False?

I often hesitate to count sessions because I didn't do it "right."	T	F
I compare myself unfavourably to others who seem more dedicated.	T	F
I've restarted parts of the practice I'd already completed.	T	F

Write a compassionate message to your perfectionistic self:

Dear Me,

_____
_____
_____
_____
_____

Communication with Loved Ones

Have you spoken with your partner or household members about your commitment? What do you want to express to them about why this practice matters to you? Or, how your practice may affect shared time or responsibilities? Now is a good time to reaffirm your relationship with them and assure them that you remain committed (if you are).

Ngondro can gradually become an integral part of how you perceive yourself, your choices, and your daily life. Over time, its rhythms, symbols, and intentions will subtly infuse your being, like a slow, steady rain. If you persevere, you'll discover that it reshapes you from the inside out.

Conclusion

In the daily flow of ngondro practice, after completing your formal session, you rise again as your self-visualized deity from the Guru Yoga. Whether that self-image is Vajrayogini, Yeshe Tsogyal, Red Troma, or another deity, the core principle remains the same. You gradually shift away from seeing yourself merely as a human being defined by your life story. Instead, you begin to uncover a pure and profound aspect of your consciousness, identifying what within you is truly deathless.

Remembering the futility of identifying solely as a being of cyclic existence, coming and going from one predicament to the next, your worries about the future will naturally lessen. Your teacher can also provide practices to help you continue this process in your sleep and dreams. Ngondro can be a continuous inner practice for you, no matter what your circumstances.

Live the teachings of Vajrayana Buddhism. Revisit them, wrestle with them, and return to unlock more layers of meaning. Look around, and step forward in your timeless, pure body of light.

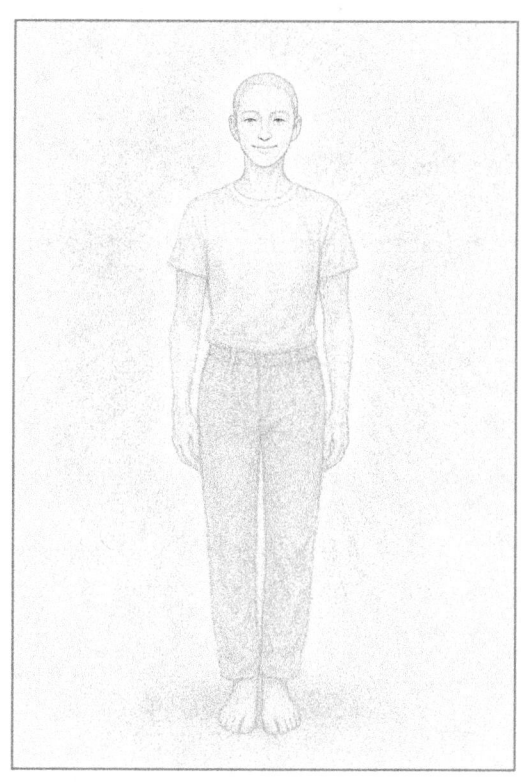

About The Author

Loppon Yudron Wangmo is an American teacher of Tibetan Buddhism who is known as a bridgebuilder between traditional practices and contemporary ways. She directs the Mayum Mountain Foundation, a California-based source of online classes and in-person small group retreats.

Her title loppon, conferred by Lama Pema Dorje Rinpoche, indicates that she is a respected teacher with a deep level of expertise gained through thirty years of in-depth practice and study. She completed a traditional cloistered three-year, three-month retreat under the guidance of Lama Tharchin Rinpoche, and shorter directed isolated retreats totaling another three under the direction of Lama Pema Dorje Rinpoche. Her mentors, along with her third main inspiration, Adzom Paylo Rinpoche, placed a strong emphasis on practice.

Loppon is the author of two Buddhist novels for teenagers, in a four-book series still in progress. She uses innovative ways to share the message of Tibetan Buddhism with different kinds of people.

Excavating Pema Ozer
The Buddha of Lightning Peak

She has an author website that you might want to check out:

yudronwangmo.com

The Mayum Mountain Foundation

Tibetan Buddhism in Our Lives

Expand your wisdom and refine your consciousness through Buddhist Practice.
At the Mayum Mountain Foundation, we aspire to be a spiritual home for those who want to integrate the practice and study of Buddhism into their lives. Our focus is on the path of personal transformation of the Nyingma School of Tibetan Buddhism. Everyone is welcome.

Mayum is a respectful word for mother in the Tibetan language. The mother is our hidden ability to find the open and free aspect of our minds, allowing limitless love and compassion to come forth. The word mountain means gaining stability in that. Practice is how we find Mayum Mountain.

We are a tax-exempt non-profit Nyingma Buddhist group based in Copperopolis, California. We provide online classes, in-person retreats, and meditations. Sign up for the newsletter on our website if you want to be kept up to date about everything we are doing.

www.mayummountain.org

www.ingramcontent.com/pod-product-compliance
Lightning Source LLC
Chambersburg PA
CBHW051354070526

44584CB00025B/3754